Shadow Work Prompts

A Guide for Healing and Self-Discovery

Preface

D o you feel like you are being held back?

Does it feel like your inner shadow is meddling in your life, stopping you from living it?

Are you struggling to move on from hurt and pain?

If yes, this is the guide for you.

Everyone should learn shadow work because everyone has a shadow self that dictates many of their feelings, actions, and words, whether they believe it or not. Hurt and pain are part of life; everyone needs to heal and learn to move on from bad experiences, whether they were from early childhood or adulthood.

Table of Contents

Preface iii

Introduction 1

Chapter 1: Your Shadow Self 3

What Is the Shadow Self? 3

How to Embrace Your Shadow Self...................... 5

Chapter 2: Getting Started with Shadow Work 10

What Is Shadow Work? 10

Shadow Work Benefits.. 11

How to Practice Shadow Work...................... 16

Shadow Work Prompts and Exercises 19

Chapter 3: Shadow Work Journaling 21

What Is a Shadow Work Journal?...................... 22

Starting a Shadow Work Journal 23

Final Thoughts 31

Journalling Tips 35

25 Shadow Journalling Prompts...................... 37

Chapter 4: Shadow Work Prompts...................40

79 Shadow Work Prompts.................. 42

Chapter 5: Shadow Work Questions.....................51

Conclusion...................60

References...................63

Introduction

On October 31st, Halloween, people dress up in terrifying costumes and head out onto the streets to scare people – in a good, fun way, of course. However, while most do this for fun, they are actually openly celebrating something that resides in everyone – macabre and darkness. They allow "evil" to reside alongside good, a duality that exists in every person.

This duality has always been a large part of many philosophies, mythologies, religions, and psychotherapies. Greek dualism relates to the soul and body, while Hinduism discusses reality's duality. Christian dualism is about God creating humans as embodied and sustaining the disembodied you between dying and being reborn. You can read plenty of modern stories based on this concept – Dr. Jekyll and Mr. Hyde is the perfect example.

If you think about it, each person has two distinct versions – the visible version, the one on show to everyone else, and the shadow self that most people rarely, if ever, experience, only catching the occasional glimpse.

The self can be likened to an iceberg. What you see is a tiny portion of who or what you are; it's you as you know it. The part hidden beneath the water is your subconscious and is much bigger; it has a presence but an unseen, quiet one. Carl Jung was responsible for coining the concept of the shadow self and also for developing the tools in use today to integrate your shadow self into your personality.

This guide will walk you through shadow selves, shadow work, and plenty of exercises and shadow prompts to help you heal yourself and go on a journey of self-discovery. It's how you learn who you really are and learn to cope with everything life throws at you.

So, if you want to learn how to heal and move on, keep reading to discover everything you need to help you.

Chapter 1:

Your Shadow Self

Nobody loves every part of themselves; everyone has some part they don't like, be it guilt, doubt, fear, or shame. These "bad" parts of yourself are known as your shadow self, but there is some good news; if you can learn to love your shadow self, your life will be more balanced and happier.

What Is the Shadow Self?

The shadow self is one or more parts of yourself that you struggle to accept, be it your thoughts, certain emotions, or personality traits. More often than not, most people shy away from even identifying these parts, let alone acknowledging or embracing them.

Why do people deny or ignore their shadow self?

Because they don't feel like these traits or qualities fit how they perceive themselves.

Let's say you strongly believe that resentment as a mother is directly related to being a bad mom or ungrateful. You don't accept or embrace the shadow self, allowing yourself to feel frustrated or angry towards your children at times or towards a situation that you see as impacting your "mom" qualities. They deny or ignore their feelings, believing they are less than they should be because of those thoughts or actions.

Carl Jung was the famous psychoanalyst who first made the idea of the shadow self popular. He believed that the shadow housed repressed feelings and thoughts, but not all are necessarily bad. Jung thought that the shadow could also hold onto positive traits; if others minimized or invalidated those thoughts and feelings, it could lead to you repressing them.

Does Everyone Have a Shadow Self?

Yes, or so Jung believed. Everyone enters the world free of judgment, but the older you get, the more experiences you have, causing you to judge yourself and others.

You receive messages, from friends, relatives, family, and even society, about what is and isn't acceptable, and you push the unacceptable things into your shadows. However, Jung also believed that the best thing you could do is learn to accept and integrate your shadow rather than reject it. He believed everyone could work through their repressed feelings and thoughts and incorporate them, leading to internal peace, rather than unconsciously allowing their shadow selves to drive their feelings and needs.

How to Embrace Your Shadow Self

You can learn to embrace your shadow self in the following ways:

1. Be a Curious Observer

Shadow work is primarily about bringing together all the parts of yourself that you have disowned, all your experiences, and you do this through intention, awareness, and curiosity. You will begin to notice themes and patterns that show up throughout your life, and the more you see your mind, the easier it will become to understand the influence you allow your shadow self to have over you.

2. Learn to be Nonjudgmental Toward Yourself

As you see your mind and shadow, learn to be non judgmental and not put yourself down. When a shadow emotion comes along, allow yourself to experience it without judgment for yourself or the feeling.

3. Team Up with a Professional

All deep healing work should be done with the help of a professional, at least when you start. Shadow work is difficult because evicting something lodged deep in your subconscious and sending it to your conscious mind by yourself is tough. It can be frightening and intense; professional help can make the path easier to follow. Make sure you team up with a nonjudgmental, caring, supportive counselor; you must feel safe with them when you explore your shadow side because you are using self-compassion to embrace your vulnerabilities.

4. Meditate

Meditation is underrated, and not enough people do it. It is one of the best ways to learn to see your mind and be nonjudgmental. Meditation practices driven by insight can help you build your consciousness and learn to accept and embrace your shadow emotions.

5. Start a Shadow Journal

Shadow journalling is highly recommended when you start doing shadow work. As with any journal, it lets you get your thoughts down on paper, thus removing them from your head and making reflection much easier. We'll be discussing journalling and prompts later in the book.

6. Engage in Past-Life Regression

But only with a professional therapist. Nontraditional therapies have their place in shadow work, and past-life regression is one of the more popular ones. There's nothing to say that some aspects of your previous lives don't affect your shadow self, especially for those who believe in karma or past lives.

Exercises and Prompts

Try the following exercises and prompts to help you start:

1. Put Labels on Your Emotional Experiences

This is a habit you must learn to get into; give your emotional experiences a detailed label in writing or via mental reflection. For example, if you feel sad, dig deeper. Ask yourself about the type of sadness you feel. Is it exhaustion, depletion, loneliness, or hopelessness? The more specific you are in labeling your emotions, the more aware you become, helping you identify what's needed to help you care for your emotional health.

2. Think of Someone Who Triggers You

Think about something that happened recently, where someone caused you frustration, irritation, or annoyance. You will find it easier to access your shadow when you can do this. Think about what bothered you about the person, whether it was something they said or did. Then reflect on your observations and think about whether they could be a reflection of something deep inside you.

Ask yourself how often you criticize yourself for the behavior that irritated you. Ask yourself if the person reminded you of another person who you feel wronged you in some way. When you can answer those questions truthfully, you might find the space to reflect more deeply and find a connection to your shadow self.

3. Ask Specific Questions to Dig Deeper

Lastly, ask yourself some thoughtful and specific questions about your shadow self. As you learn to see and accept your shadow, try asking these questions:

- Are my thoughts real or critical statements about me, a relationship, a situation, or an interaction I experienced?
- Was I allowed to feel my shadow emotions when I was younger? Or was I judged and made to feel ashamed of having those experiences? Was I punished for them?
- What messages did I receive when I experienced a certain emotion?
- Have I learned to ignore or avoid my shadow emotions because I wasn't supported earlier in life?
- When I tried to share my feelings with a significant other, was I met with anger?

Everyone has a shadow self, but learning to embrace and integrate it won't be easy. However, the hard work is worth it. When you learn to accept your shadow self, you create the space you need to understand your experiences and process them, thus leading to healing and positive change.

Chapter 2:

Getting Started with Shadow Work

While the shadow self typically contains all your negative emotions, thoughts, and feelings, like anger, resentment, and sadness, it can also contain positive things. According to Jung, the shadow self is integral to your world experiences and relationships. He also said that when you learn to work with your shadow self, you can better understand yourself and lead a more balanced life.

What Is Shadow Work?

The concept of shadow work comes from the concept of the shadow self, originating from Jungian psychology. Jung said that personalities contain persona, the part of your personality the public sees, and the shadow self, the part you keep hidden or private. Whereas the persona is always on show, the shadow self is where you hide the traits you don't want anyone else to see.

That said, the shadow self should never be considered shameful or negative because it is a critical part of who you are.

Shadow work aims to assimilate your persona and shadow to help you learn to manage impulses and feelings you would normally ignore, such as greed or anger.

Jung also believed that your shadow self is influenced by collective unconsciousness, a Jungian idea referring to society's collective impulses and memories. This also results in systemic issues fitting into your shadow self, such as racism.

Shadow work can help you confront the bits of your personality you try to keep hidden, the parts you ignore. It can also help you address impulses and prejudices that come from broader society.

Shadow Work Benefits

The shadow self is a concept that can't be tangibly measured. It is subjective and dependent on context. For example, where one culture may accept something, another may consider it taboo, affecting whether it becomes part of your shadow self.

Because of this, little scientific research exists on how effective shadow work is. Instead, the research typically focuses on how to use shadow work to solve certain challenges in your life.

Take a paper published in 2022 by Rachel Newsome, for example. This argued that a person could use creative writing to help them process trauma and that they should draw on Jung's understanding of the unconscious.

Some practitioners say that their shadow work has helped them in the following ways:

- To identify negative personal traits and negative traits instilled in them by society and counteract them
- To accept themselves more easily
- To understand that other people face challenges with their shadow selves
- To confront challenging emotions, such as grief and trauma
- To understand how childhood, society, and relationships have influenced their interactions and lives.

Sometimes, parts of the shadow self are the motivating force behind good acts. For example, if you can confront implicit biases you normally try to ignore, you may find it easier to change them.

In the same way, if you are more aware of your anger, it can help you channel it for a good cause, such as fighting for a cause you truly believe in.

Other benefits include:

- **Confidence and Self-Esteem:** shadow work allows you to be more confident because you are the full version of who you are; your persona AND shadow self. It can help you remove self-doubt you might normally keep hidden, self-doubt about parts of you that you've kept hidden or tried to ignore, thus boosting your confidence in achieving your goals.
- **Creativity:** your shadow hides traits that others consider bad, but it can also hide your creative side. When you learn to accept your shadow, you can embrace that creativity. Rather than keeping your darker self hidden, you can tap into all your unique expressions.
- **Better Relationships:** when you learn to accept who you are and love yourself, you gain

the space you need to accept and love others for who they are rather than as projections of the part of you that you dislike.

- **Self-Acceptance:** shadow work helps you eliminate the self-hatred you hold onto, be it subconsciously. The only way to do that is to fully accept both sides of you and learn how to be self-aware. When you accept your shadow as part of you, you accept and have compassion for all aspects of yourself.
- **Hidden Talents:** you don't have just one shadow self; you also have a "golden shadow," your inner resources and strengths that you might not have realized you had. Learning shadow work can help you uncover this extra shadow, especially when you fear that your shadow self is too dark. Most of the time, it's your golden shadow taking up the bulk of the space, but it has never been given the opportunity it needs to thrive. When you learn and practice shadow work, you can draw your golden shadow into the light and throw yourself wholeheartedly into everything you can and want to do.

- **Overall Wellness:** when you repress your shadow, it can lead to many different problems. You might not even associate these problems with a side of you that you repressed, at least not until you are ready to accept and embrace your shadow. Practicing shadow work can help you control your journey to wellness because it tackles the root causes. Rather than focusing on a specific issue, such as an unhealthy relationship or anxiety, it goes straight to the root of the problem.

- **Increased Compassion:** most people are guilty of projection when interacting with others, and shadow work can help you reduce this. With practice, you will find yourself less likely to let other people's quirks and personality traits trigger you and begin to feel more empathy and compassion for others. You will no longer project your dark side onto them but will see them as whole, people who are likely facing their own battles and challenges.

- **Better Clarity:** shadow work gives you more clarity in how your feelings, thoughts, and emotions dictate your actions. When you understand this, you can be more authentic with better clarity.

- **Better Understanding of Human Nature:** everyone finds it easy sometimes to be self-deceitful and to label things as "right," "wrong," "good," or "bad" to suppress the inner world's full nature. With shadow work, you can reveal a clearer picture showing dark and light capabilities.

How to Practice Shadow Work

Because shadow work isn't commonly practiced, few people are trained in it. It starts with you being willing to explore your shadow self, even if it makes you uncomfortable or scares you. Some of the best strategies include:

- **Dream Analysis:** dreams were highly valued by Jung and his followers as tools to access the shadow self and the unconscious. Log your dreams and look for repetition in dreams and symbols to see whether they symbolize an aspect of your mind you might be trying to ignore.

- **Shadow Journal:** journaling is a helpful way of allowing a person access to their unconscious desires and thoughts by looking for themes and patterns. You can do this by following prompts, writing about your day, telling a story, or participating in free association.

- **Psychoanalysis:** Jung said psychoanalysis was the best way to explore your shadow self. When you enter psychoanalytic psychotherapy, you work with an analyst to help you interpret dream archetypes and unconscious symbols and uncover the motives behind your actions.

- **Sand Tray Therapy:** this type of therapy uses sand trays to promote mindfulness, encouraging you to create a scene that depicts your inner life as accurately as possible. This can help you explore your shadow self and unconscious mind.

Be aware that doing shadow work alone may not always be possible. If you are traumatized or have serious concerns about your mental health, you must seek support from a professional.

Shadow Work for Beginners

Jungian psychology says you must engage a psychoanalyst to help you with your shadow work and walk you through your shadow self. If you are just starting, you might find it best to speak to a trained practitioner in shadow work; you may have to do some searching, though, as it isn't a common practice.

Other beginner's tips include:
- Take it slowly; there's no rush
- Be mindful; shadow work isn't easy, and it can upset you
- Practice self-care and compassion, especially when faced with unexpected feelings or thoughts
- Approach your shadow self with a curious and accepting mindset

Shadow work is only one way to explore what you perceive as undesirable or shameful characteristics or traits. Other therapies, such as CBT (Cognitive Behavioral Therapy), can help you understand your self-perceptions.

Shadow Work Prompts and Exercises

These exercises are designed to help you focus on bringing what you kept hidden into the light. If you want to start off by yourself, consider the following journaling prompts:

- What are the things you most fear people finding out about you?
- Have you ever felt ashamed? Why?
- What are your strongest triggers? Where do you think those triggers come from?
- What negative thoughts or self-images do you have?
- What thoughts about others go through your head when you are angry at another person?
- What do your dreams tell you about your insecurities and fears?

Shadow Work in Spirituality

Many types of spirituality have come under the influence of shadow work, including some New Age beliefs and astrology. Some people think that, when they do shadow work, they will be spiritually awakened or create a connection with one or more spiritual worlds.

Even Jung never ruled out spirituality's influence on the psyche, despite many of his theories focusing on biological reasons as to why humans behave and think as they do. Over time, Jung's ideas have become combined with other belief systems, which means there isn't one single model of shadow work linked to spirituality.

Chapter 3:

Shadow Work Journaling

Journaling has long been heralded as a way of digging deep into memories and emotions, especially those that could be holding you down and stopping you from moving forward.

Whether you are new to shadow work or an old hand, journaling can help you gain access to your past to work through issues and move past them. Writing your feelings and thoughts down on paper is cathartic, sometimes more so than talking.

This is very useful when you need to work through traumatic experiences in your past, experiences that stop you from getting on with your life. When you write your feelings down, it can almost feel like you are dragging all the toxicity out of your head and putting it on paper, a written version of Dumbledore's Pensive, if you like Harry Potter.

Journaling can also help you see themes and patterns in your life. Let's say that something bad always happens when you go on vacation. Or you reply in a snarky manner whenever someone asks you how you are. By writing everything down in your journal, you can see these patterns and learn to work with them to bring positivity back to your life.

What Is a Shadow Work Journal?

Shadow work journals are no different from any other journal in that you write your thoughts and feelings. The difference is that when you write in your shadow journal, you focus on your shadow aspects, what you keep hidden, and bring them into the light. When you write your feelings down, you can begin to understand the parts of you that you try to hide and ignore. In time, negative patterns will diminish to the point where they no longer have a negative effect on your life. Whether hand-written or digital, journaling can help you learn to understand yourself.

Why You Should Use a Journal

Journaling helps you understand the parts of you that you try to avoid. It helps you acknowledge what makes you feel uncomfortable about your-self and what you want to deny or avoid looking at.

When you write these things down, you are forced to acknowledge your shadow self, accept it exists, and verbalize your thoughts.

Another benefit is that journaling helps you form a structured way to work with your shadow self, especially for those starting inner work for the first time. It makes your problems tangible, thus telling your brain that these things can be worked with and that you can change them. Not only that, but journaling your journey through your shadow work can help you track it as you go and look for connections later.

When you write about your shadow work, you allow yourself to reflect on your life, what's happening now, and what happened in the past. It allows you to see how everything is connected, how far you have traveled, and whether your actions are doing any good – are they helping you work through what holds you back?

Starting a Shadow Work Journal

You can start a shadow work journal in many ways, including a notebook and pen, a document on your computer, or even a smartphone or tablet app.

There are plenty of digital journaling services you can use, such as Evernote or Day One, but however you choose to do it, make sure it is a place and way to write your thoughts down and process them.

Once you have chosen your method, open your journal and begin writing; it's no more difficult than that. You don't need to be a professional writer; just write down everything. Start with what comes into your mind, choose one of the journal prompts in this book, or write about something that happened to you during the day. It's your choice, but, whatever you write, make sure you reflect on it and make it count.

Using Shadow Prompts

You can use the prompts in this book or write your own; the choice is yours. However, starting with pre-written ones is recommended for beginners, so long as they are right for you.

Some prompts will ask you to look further than others and may make you uncomfortable. Remember that when a prompt makes you feel this way, it's because it is dragging something important to the surface that you need to work on. Make sure you give such prompts space, think about them carefully, and write down anything and everything that comes into your mind. Allow things to unfold in a natural order, and don't let things get stuck in a loop of shame and self-judgment.

Shadow work requires self-care, especially when you have finished a session. It's the only way to process what comes up and calm yourself. Recommended methods include meditation, a walk, or anything else that makes you happy, so long as it is self-care.

Working with Pre-Written Prompts

It's very easy to overlook that when a shadow prompt makes you feel uncomfortable, it's a good one. It makes you uncomfortable because it gets under your skin and focuses on something important. The more uncomfortable you feel, the better the prompt is at doing what it's meant to – help you work through and overcome the negative thoughts holding you back. You need to heal and move on; the only way to do that is to face what's stopping you.

You may not realize that your thoughts are negative, at least not consciously, so be open in your approach and willing to change your perspective if necessary.

Doing Shadow Work Alone

Most people think that shadow work should be done with a professional; this is recommended if you are a beginner or have suffered trauma. However, some shadow work can be done alone, and most people can do it quite easily. All you need is an open mind, and you must be prepared to challenge everything you ever thought. Done right, you can learn to live with who you are and be happy in your life.

It is often said that shadow work is nothing more than facing your demons, and yes, for some people, that's exactly what it is. However, even if you haven't suffered trauma, you can still benefit from it, especially if you want to become self-aware and learn about yourself.

Shadow work is all about facing the parts of yourself you keep hidden, examining your shame and pain, pulling it out of the dark, and looking at it from all angles until it makes sense.

This process can be divided into four steps:

1. Identify

It isn't easy to identify your shadow self, but you need to understand that you have one, that it is part of you, which means it can change you.

The first step to getting past the fear of identifying your shadow self is to work out where you are right now, at the moment. What do you feel? How do you feel? What thoughts are running through your mind? What, if any, beliefs have you got about yourself?

Once you have done that, give names to your feelings and emotions. These include anger, shame, guilt, sadness, inadequacy, resentment, fear of abandonment, etc. When you draw up your list and give each one a name, you will find it easier to see how each one affects you daily and why you may be experiencing them.

2. Accept and Embrace

When you can embrace your shadow self, it means that you accept your emotions – all of them, not just the ones you want to accept. Be gentle – when you deal with negative emotions, it can make you feel bad, and it often comes from how you dealt with them in the past. Don't beat yourself up or force yourself. You should be self-compassionate but don't let it stop you from being honest about how you feel and what you are experiencing.

When expressing emotions, it's very easy for us to label each one as good or bad. However, that's one of the worst things you can do. Emotions are nothing more than energy, and, good or bad, each has its own value. When we learn to see that each emotion has a place, we can begin to see that everything about us is useful, making up who we are, even the parts we don't like.

Accept that these parts of you exist.

Shadow work encourages you to look at those parts and see them as part of you, not as something you should keep hidden away. As your work progresses, you will learn how these negative traits interact with the positives and their effect on your life – they do affect you, whether you realize it or not, but it's usually subconscious. Once you see how every part of you interacts, you can learn to build a happier, more balanced life.

Let's say you tend to get angry, sometimes quite quickly. Rather than hiding it or trying to control it as you normally do, shadow work can help you learn to consider anger as a positive way of expressing your emotions and feelings about an unfair or unjust situation. This can help you understand that anger is a part of you; it's part of what makes you who you are, not something you need to hide away or fix.

3. Understand

When you accept that your whole self is made up of negative and positive traits and that a certain trait resides within you, you can learn to accept that it doesn't need to be controlled or fixed. Ask yourself how that trait serves you at the current time. For example, ask yourself, "Does my anger give me power?" "Does fear keep me safe?"

It could be that something triggered those feelings in you, perhaps a work-related problem, or you could just be having an off day. You need to understand where your emotions are rooted; when you know where they come from, you can learn to process them and bring them into the whole of you without feeling guilty or ashamed.

You can understand where your feelings come from in several ways. Ask yourself, "What does this feeling make me want?" Alternatively, ask for advice from a close friend; ask how they would respond if they were in the same situation.

Sometimes, you may respond because of your beliefs; other times, it may be because of something that triggers memories of the past.

Be brave; figure out the why behind your feelings and emotions.

4. Integrate

When you see yourself as a whole, your shadow self may overwhelm you. You see everything you wish was different about you and want to hide it all away. But doing that means you are fighting yourself, and when you do that, it leads to issues in other parts of your life.

When you learn to see your shadow self as a part of you and not an accumulation of what you don't like, you can begin to change your life for the better. You can work on those parts, work with them and not against them, by asking questions like these:

- What does this part of me need?
- How do I support it?
- How does this part want to be seen?
- What does this part want to accomplish in my life?

You need to determine how to work with your shadow self and not against it; that's the only way to live a better, happier life.

Final Thoughts

Here are some final considerations about your shadow work:

Have an Open Mind

The shadow work process will help you empty your subconscious, allowing you to be free and live a life of acceptance and happiness. It isn't easy to do, but it's totally worth it. These three tips can help you get a handle on your mindset:

- **Be Honest and Authentic:** it may feel uncomfortable to start with because it can be quite scary to start digging deep into your psyche, looking for answers about who you are. However, when you can be honest and authentic with yourself, the better off you will be long term.

- **Allow Yourself to Be Judgement-Free in Exploring Your Psyche:** shadow work requires you to look at the "ugly" parts of you, such as your insecurities, fear, and anger.

However, you should not stop yourself from exploring all these parts of yourself. We all have a shadow self; it is part of us. So long as no one gets hurt by your explorations, go ahead and dig deep but be honest and open as you do so.

- **Challenge Your Opinions and Beliefs:** regardless of how strong you hold them, you should never be afraid of challenging your own beliefs and opinions. Remember, while a belief or thought may feel real at the time, it isn't necessarily always going to be true or real. Step outside your comfort zone; you might be quite surprised at what you discover about yourself.

Be Cautious in Your Shadow Work

While you can do your shadow work alone, it isn't easy, especially if you want to heal and grow. It takes a large amount of two things you might not realize you have – courage and strength. However, it can also be dangerous if you don't do it right.

When you start, take your time. Don't rush into exploring what you might struggle to handle, especially at the start; you will only make things worse and could do yourself serious emotional and mental harm.

Take time between sessions to process what you learned and ensure you are okay. Only handle one thing at a time and deal with one issue before you move on to the next.

When you start exploring your shadow, it's very easy to become lost. However, you must remember that you have needs and feelings; push yourself too hard, and you might only succeed in making things worse for yourself.

You should never consider shadow work as a quick way to fix things. It takes a lot of patience and time, so make sure you look after yourself and ask for support if you struggle.

Work Your Method Out

You don't need to do shadow work every day, although you can if you want to. The key to success is approaching shadow work journaling in a way that works for you. Some people like to use a journal or notebook to write down their thoughts, while others prefer to use art or drawings. Some even like to use music.

One method might be more helpful to you than others, but you should maintain an open mind. Be observant, and take note of what works for you, of what brings the results you want.

Shadow work is important in the healing process because it lets you face and accept your demons; that's the only way to work with them. You mustn't rush this process, and definitely don't keep putting it off; if you don't do it now, you may never get to it. Shadow work is for life; as you grow into the person you are meant to be, the process will grow with you.

Everyone deals with their shadows in their own way, be it using a journal or talking about things with someone who understands where you are coming from. There are no rules; you just need an open mind and be willing to try something new until you find what works for you.

A Rewarding Experience

If you have picked this book up, you are already aware that being human comes with certain hardships. Everyone struggles with pain and fear at times, but by the same token, every person has the capacity to be amazing.

Inside you is an incredible person that deserves the blessings life brings. You can only recognize that person if you take the time to understand them.

Shadow work is a deeper level of self-reflection than most are willing to face. You must be consistent and courageous in facing your issues and understanding who you really are. Shadow work can help you tread forwards in life, carrying more awareness that teaches you how to deal with issues instead of hiding them; facing them to help you grow.

Journalling Tips

The primary goal of shadow work is to become aware of your shadow self, to become conscious of it, and accept it as part of you. One of the best ways is to use your shadow journal. Use it to mirror your thoughts and give you a place to process everything.

Here are some final tips to help you:

1. Start Slow and Small

Shadow work isn't meant to be lighthearted. It is hard work, personal, and intimate, and can sap your energy. When you first start, don't be too ambitious. When you sit down to write in your journal, set a timer for 10 minutes and, when the time is up, stop. Start again tomorrow or when you are next scheduled to do shadow work.

2. Use Journalling Prompts

There is no need to be the leader and practitioner of your shadow work journalling. Think about using prompts. You shouldn't put yourself under pressure to think about what to process; prompts are one of the best ways to help you direct your thoughts and energy during practice so you can confront your shadow.

3. Celebrate Personal Growth

Celebration is an incredibly important part of journaling for personal growth. Looking inside yourself and examining what you've tried to keep hidden is not easy, whether you have consciously or unconsciously kept things locked away. Journalling and reflection should be considered progress, and it's part of the process designed to help you trust your findings and process what you learn. That should be celebrated, so don't hold back.

4. Talk to a Friend or Therapist

This is optional and is wholly dependent on you, but it can help some people to share what they learn with others. If you need to talk to process what you learn, it can help if you have someone who will listen to you and help you stay on your chosen path. It could be a close, trusted friend or a therapist; whoever you choose, letting someone else in can help you in your journey of healing and self-discovery.

25 Shadow Journalling Prompts

Shadow work journaling is useful for recording past experiences, exploring your memories, jotting down the stories that make your life, and unpacking your belief systems. Writing these things down is cathartic and powerful, and while I will dedicate the next chapter to plenty of prompts, here are 25 to get you started:

1. Who influences me and my decisions the most?

2. What is my worst trait? Why do I think that?

3. What was one of the biggest challenges I faced as a child, and how is it affecting my life today?

4. What situations make me want to gloss over the truth?

5. What was the biggest trouble I got into when I was a kid?
6. What situations trigger me the most? Why?
7. Who has hurt or betrayed me? What are my feelings about that person?
8. What are my happiest, most joyful memories?
9. What are my worst, most shameful memories?
10. What do people think of me, and is it accurate?
11. When was I last disappointed, and why?
12. When do I feel I am valued the most?
13. Which relationships have helped me the most in my life?
14. What hard feelings do I want to let go of but struggle to?
15. What must I forgive myself for?
16. How do I feel when someone compliments me?
17. What do I regret the most in my life so far?
18. What are my beliefs about myself?
19. What is the worst trait a person could have?

20. What does having healthy boundaries with a person thing look like?
21. What emotions or feelings do I hide?
22. What do I want to change about myself?
23. What do I judge others for, and why?
24. Who can I rely on for advice or support, and how often do I turn to them?
25. What makes me feel trapped, and how do I define freedom

Chapter 4:

Shadow Work Prompts

This chapter is dedicated to prompts you can use to get started on your shadow work journaling and are useful for beginners. Some may feel a little bit repetitive, but that is how they are intended to be – that way, they dig into your subconscious and tease out things you might think are hidden deep.

Write the answers to these questions in as much detail as you can remember. You may not remember much, but the more you do your shadow work, the more you will remember, so repeat them daily for two weeks.

You might find yourself remembering things when you are not doing your shadow work; keep your journal with you and write down what you remember as soon as you do or as soon after.

1. List everything about you that bothers you. For example, "I hate that I can't seem to keep my house free of clutter."

2. List everything you feel guilty about. For example, "I feel guilty that I don't tidy up the mess."

3. List everything you are scared of. For example, "I'm scared that people will judge me because my house is cluttered."

4. List everything about yourself you wish was different. For example, "I wish I wasn't messy."

5. List everything you want other people to change. For example, "I wish my friend/ brother/sister wasn't so messy."

6. List everything that makes you feel resentful or angry. For example, "I'm angry at myself because I'm lazy."

7. List everything you do that makes you feel bad about yourself. For example, "I feel bad that my house is always so cluttered and messy."

8. List the things that you wish were different about others. For example, "I wish my family respected me more."

9. List the ways that you hurt others, even though you don't mean to. For example, "I

often say something without thinking, even though I know it's hurtful."

10. List the things that make you feel ashamed of yourself. For example, "I'm ashamed of letting my friends or family see all the clutter and mess in my house."

11. List everything you are frightened of admitting, be it to others or yourself. For example, "I'm scared of admitting how messy my house seems to be."

When you have listed everything, take some time to read it all back and reflect on it all. Think about what it all means to you and why any of it bothers you. What would your life be like if you didn't fear anything?

Repeat this for two weeks.

79 Shadow Work Prompts

Print this list of prompts, pin it where you can see it, and refer to it when necessary.

1. What emotion do I most try to avoid feeling? How does it make me react when I feel that emotion?

2. What negative emotion am I comfortable with the most? Do I like this emotion so much because it feels normal and right to me?
3. Is my inner voice critical or kind? What does it say to me the most often?
4. Is it truly my inner voice, or do others influence it, like my friends or family?
5. How do I feel other people see me, and how does that make me feel?
6. How do I want others to see me? Does this differ from how I feel they see me?
7. When am I at my most judgmental?
8. Which of my relationships should have stronger boundaries, and what stops me from setting them?
9. Do I respect the boundaries other people set?
10. What are my core values?
11. Is my life aligned with those values? If not, which ones am I not respecting
12. Do I share the same or similar core values with my family? Does that make me happy? If not, where did I get those values from?

13. When did I last feel disappointed? Was it right for me to feel that way? Could something else have been responsible for the feeling?

14. When did I feel betrayed by someone? What would I say to them now?

15. Is there a trait I see in others that I wish I had? What is it?

16. How often do I overthink things I have done or said? Why do I think I do this?

17. What triggers my jealousy? Why do I think this happens?

18. What first tells me that my mental health is not good?

19. Do other people's opinions sway me? Why/why not?

20. Do I value myself? Do I value what I bring to life and the world?

21. Have I ever done anything that made someone else proud? Who were they? Why did their thoughts matter so much?

22. Imagine I am on my deathbed. What is the biggest regret I fear having?

23. What do I wish others understood better about me? Can I share that part of me with them?

24. What leaves an empty feeling inside me? How do I try to fill up the void, and could I do it in healthier ways?

25. Who influences me the most? Am I okay with it?

26. What does freedom mean to me?

27. Write down when I am hard on myself. Why do I think I am hard on myself?

28. Describe what failure means to me. Am I scared of failure? Why/why not?

29. What is the relationship between my parents and me like? Has it changed from when I was a child?

30. What is the relationship between my siblings and me like? Has it changed from when we were all younger?

31. Describe what achievement means to me. Do I celebrate when I achieve something?

32. Do I believe I can only be as good as my last achievement?

33. What would I be if I could be whatever I wanted? Am I working towards being that person? Why/why not?
34. Do I think I have tried to fit in with others by sacrificing who I am? Why?
35. Do I feel superior to my peers in any part of my life? What part? Am I really superior?
36. What gives me purpose in life? Can I do more to improve my purpose?
37. Would I change anything about those closest to me? What? Could I change something about myself to strengthen these relationships?
38. Do I feel valued?
39. What makes me feel valued?
40. Do I think I am confrontational? Am I proud of this, or would I prefer to be more agreeable?
41. Write down how I see myself. Do I like what I have written?
42. What traits can I see in me that reminds me of my parents?

43. How did I feel when I discovered my parents weren't perfect? Does it help me accept that I am also not perfect?

44. Is there someone I have never forgiven? Has this affected my life? How? Can I forgive that person now?

45. When I was younger, how did I process emotions?

46. When someone oversteps my boundaries, how does it make me feel? How do I react?

47. What would I like to change about myself? Why? Has someone told me that I should change things about myself?

48. How do I define perfect? Can I attain perfection?

49. Do I hold myself to a higher standard than others?

50. In what ways do I show up for others that I don't show up for myself?

51. What do I feel the most guilt about in my life so far? Why? Is it something I can make peace with?

52. What do I feel the most ashamed about in my life so far? Why? Is it something I can forgive myself for?

53. When did I feel the most alone in my life? Why?

54. What is my biggest regret in my life so far? Why?

55. Did I ever stay in a relationship that wasn't good for me? Why?

56. Have I ever been scared of making a commitment? Why did I feel like that?

57. Did I ever feel that I had an unhealthy attachment to someone? What made me feel that way?

58. How would it make me feel to live the rest of my life in the way I have lived so far? What would I do differently, if anything?

59. Do I feel equal to others? Or do I feel less or more than equal? Why?

60. Which personality trait do I most hate being described with? Why?

61. When did I last feel someone belittled my emotions? How did I react, and could I have reacted better?

62. What emotions bring the worst out in me?

63. When do I put a mask on and allow a different persona to take center stage? Is it only in certain situations or with certain people? What do I think would happen if I showed my true self?

64. What traits do I have that I don't like? Are there any vulnerabilities behind them? Could I replace them with more productive, positive traits?

65. How do I respond when someone pays me a compliment? Why do I respond in this way?

66. What's the biggest lie I tell myself?

67. What's the biggest promise to myself I've ever broken? How did it make me feel?

68. What's the biggest promise to someone else I have ever broken? How did it make me feel?

69. Have I ever knowingly manipulated someone? Why? Was I trying to meet one of my needs?

70. Have I ever felt as though someone has taken advantage of me? How did it make me feel?

71. What is my deepest source of anger?

72. Which relationships no longer help or serve me? Can I salvage them, or should I let them go?

73. What do I want to stop running from? Is there a way I could face it head-on?

74. What was the last unkind thought I had? Did I voice it, or did it stay in my head?

75. What situation in my life so far do I wish had a different outcome?

76. Am I dramatic? Why/why not?

77. Do I feel comfortable asking for help? Why/why not?

78. What makes me feel unsafe?

79. Who do I feel I have let down the most in my life? Why?

Chapter 5:

Shadow Work Questions

When you are comfortable with the prompts in the last chapter and are happy to continue, you might want to start digging a little deeper. You might decide you want to explore deeper into your subconscious to see what else you can learn. Make sure you do the previous prompts for at least two weeks before you attempt this; you don't want to dig too deeply right at the start.

The prompts below are designed to widen your exploration of your subconscious.

1. What are some of the common gripes and complaints I have? Where do they originate?
2. Have I stopped progressing in a certain area of my life because someone once told me it wasn't important?
3. Have I suppressed a habit to ensure I fit in and am more like others?
4. What vices do I have? Do they meet my needs? How? For example, drinking makes

me feel less guilty; coffee stops me from feeling lazy; sugary foods make me feel safer, etc.

5. Has my dishonesty hurt others or myself? When?

6. What irritates me in other people? What makes me angry? Have I ever shown that trait? Has my partner? How has this influenced me? Does it remind me of a past event?

7. How do I react when complimented? Do I brush it off or bask in glory just a little too much? Is this because I didn't feel appreciated as a child? What event triggered it

8. List five to eight memories from my childhood in as much detail as possible. Why do I still remember them so vividly?

9. What one event in my life do I regret the most? If I could, which event would I completely wipe out of my life?

10. Talk about childhood traumas. How do they affect my behavior now?

11. What about traumas in my teenage years? What were they, and are they affecting me now

12. What do I struggle with the most in my life? How long have I been struggling with it? Do

I have any limiting beliefs surrounding this issue? What are they?

13. When I am angry, what do I do? How do I react? Is this a healthy reaction? Why/why not?

14. Am I a good person? Why/why not?

15. What wounded my inner child the deepest?

16. What would I say to my younger self if I could talk to them? What would I tell them? What advice would I give?

17. Which of my dreams have I not fulfilled? How did they influence me, and how do they affect my life now?

18. Which of my parents was I/am I closest to? How did they influence who I am now?

19. Am I aggressive? Have I ever hurt anyone with my aggression? How much?

20. What event in my life caused me the most embarrassment? How did it affect me?

21. When I meet people for the first time, do I judge them? How do I determine the parameters of my judgment? Why do I judge others on certain aspects?

22. What makes me jealous of another person? Why am I jealous? Was this insecurity

triggered by something that happened in the past?

23. When did I feel that an adult completely betrayed me as a child?

24. What are my core values? Have they changed or grown over time? Are they more stringent or more flexible?

25. Do I think I am becoming more like a family member? Who? Did I expect this to happen? How do I feel about it?

26. Who was the last person I argued with? Did I start the argument? What was it about?

27. How do I see self-care? How often do I practice it? If I don't do it very often, why not? What's more important to me than self-care?

28. When I am faced with a challenge, what is my first reaction?

29. What issues do I have at work? What are my patterns?

30. What is my relationship with gratitude like? Do I feel it often or express it? Why not? If I do, where did the habit come from?

31. What triggers do I have that I know about?

32. What part of me do I try to keep hidden from others, even my partner or family?

33. What emotions do I struggle to express? Where did I learn that?

34. Do I hold grudges against anyone? Why can't I forgive them?

35. Do I feel misunderstood, that no one truly understands me?

36. Am I often the victim during my self-talk? Does life happen, or do I need to make it happen?

37. Am I happy with my life right now? How could I make it better?

38. Do I feel safe being myself most of the time? If not, why not?

39. Do I find it easy to forgive myself? Does guilt weigh me down?

40. What is my deepest fear? Can I share it with someone to get some help to overcome it?

41. What is my biggest regret in life so far?

42. What promises have I made myself, and have I kept them?

43. What is the meaning of life, according to me?

44. What, if any, parts of my life am I in denial about?

45. When did I last let myself down? How did I move on?

46. What emotions do I try to avoid feeling? Be gentle with yourself with this one; it may take a bit of time for you to realize and accept them

47. What makes me nostalgic?

48. What past trauma do I struggle to let go of? How does it affect me and my life?

49. Why do I want to do shadow work? What do I think I will gain from it?

50. Have I ever had my heart broken? When? How did I deal with it and recover? What emotions could I not face?

51. Do I set boundaries in my relationships and enforce them? Why/why not? Have I always done this?

52. How do I define happiness?

53. Have I ever been a hypocrite? When?

54. Can I tell the difference between my needs and wants?

55. How do I show myself kindness?

56. Who has had the most influence over me in my life? How has their influence shaped me?

57. What do I believe it means to be truly free?

58. When did I last feel recognized and valued?

59. Did I ever have a relationship that I turned my back on and walked away from? What was it? Why did I walk away?

60. How do I define success?

61. How do I define failure?

62. Which of my relationships are no longer working and are a liability?

63. What recurring nightmares and dreams do I have?

64. How do I let myself down now? How did I let myself down in the past?

65. What does my self-talk sound like? If someone spoke to me like I talked to myself, would I be friends with them?

66. What was I most scolded for as a child?

67. What is my worst side?

68. Do I allow others to trample me emotionally? Have I ever been someone else's emotional doormat?

69. What do I most look forward to in the future?

70. When was the last time I manipulated another person? How did it make me feel?

71. Can I ask for help from friends and family when I need it? Do others ask me for help? How does helping others make me feel?

72. How do I take criticism? When did someone last criticize me? How did I react?

73. What am I most grateful for in my life?

74. Have my relationships with friends and family evolved over the last five or ten years? Are you closer or further apart? Why?

75. When did another person abandon or deceive you?

76. Was it my responsibility to look after someone when I was younger?

77. Do I believe that money can make me happy and solve all my problems?

78. What I do if money wasn't an issue? Where would I be?

79. What relationship do I have with my physical self?

80. How do I feel about giving back? How often do I give to society?
81. What one thing would have made a difference in your life when you were a child?
82. What have you been waiting to hear all your life? Who from? Why is hearing it so important?

Conclusion

Thank you for reading to the end. By now, you should have identified what you need to know about your shadow self and are now ready to integrate it into yourself and accept it.

It's important to understand your shadow self does not define you. However, it is part of you, and it thrives on unacceptance. If you feel angry, frightened, or guilty about your shadow self, it will burrow deeper and hide from you. Shine a light on it, bring it out of the shadows, and treat it with the respect and love it deserves, and your shadow self will begin to be integrated. However, this is not easy to do; it is complex and will take a great deal of time to master, not to mention effort, and it isn't a one-off. You will have to work at this for the rest of your life, but it will become second nature with practice.

When you succeed at integrating your shadow, negativity will no longer affect you. Those mistakes you made in the past? You won't make them again. You won't date the wrong type of person because you know your personality, and you will know when your shadow self begins to dictate what you do and say and how you feel, all be it subconsciously.

Integrating the shadow self is not easy and will most certainly show you the unpleasant side of yourself you strive to ignore. When you are not broken, loving yourself is hard, but it's harder still when you are. You must learn to care for your shadow self, learn creative ways to express it, and if you can't care for it, learn to carry it.

Acknowledge the existence of your shadow self and live your life knowing it is there. Do this until you come to the realization that you can both hate and love it, laugh about it and find healthy ways to express it.

Forgiveness and Kindness

Shadow work requires you to be kind to yourself. You will likely face unpleasant and intense emotions throughout the process but you must push through them with kindness and love. Treat yourself as you would treat your child. Forgive yourself for anything you have done or said. If you have wronged someone or others have wronged you, forgiveness is the best way to help your shadow self integrate and help you move forward.

Work through this guide as many times as you need to. It isn't a read-it-once-and-forget-it type of guide; it is one you can read as many times as necessary and refer back to whenever you need a prompt or two.

I hope you enjoyed this book and found it useful, and I want to wish you the absolute best in life going forward.

References

"A Beginner's Guide to Shadow Work (with 80+ Prompts)." *Lifeism.co*, lifeism.co/shadow-work-guide-and-prompts#shadow-work-prompts.

"How to Embrace & Integrate Your Shadow Self for Major Healing." *Mindbodygreen*, November 11th 2021, www.mindbodygreen.com/articles/shadow-self.

How to Start Shadow Work Journal? A Comprehensive Guide with a 7-Step Workflow - the Grey Havens. May 15th 2022, thegreyhavens.eu/how-to-start-shadow-work-journal/.

Jay, Caitey. "80 Free Shadow Work Journal Prompts for a More Authentic Life." *Caitey Jay*, May 31st 2022, www.caiteyjay.com/shadow-work-journal-prompts/.

"Shadow Work Journal." *Shadow Work Journal*, www.shadowworkjournal.app/.

"Shadow Work Journaling - What, Why & How to Do It." *Silk + Sonder*, www.silkandsonder.com/blogs/news/shadow-work-journaling-what-why-how-to-do-it.

"What Is Shadow Work? Benefits and Exercises." *Www.medicalnewstoday.com*, August 30th 2022, www.medicalnewstoday.com/articles/what-is-shadow-work#summary.

9 798215 801086